Our Nation's Capital

Washington, DC

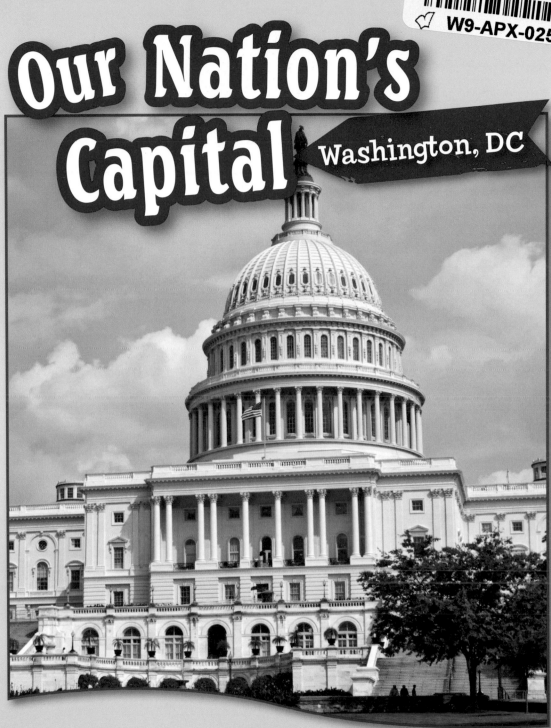

Kelly Rodgers

THE BRYANT LIBRARY
2 PAPER MILL ROAD
ROSLYN, NY 11576-2193

W9-APX-025

Consultant

Caryn Williams, M.S.Ed.
Madison County Schools
Huntsville, AL

Image Credits: Cover & p.1 Boris Suvak/Alamy; p.29 (bottom) David R. Frazier Photolibrary, Inc./Alamy; p.29 (top) Michael Ventura/Alamy; p.5 (top) Mira/Alamy; pp.4–5 Visions of America, LLC/Alamy; p.6 The Bridgeman Art; pp.20, 32 Andy Dunaway/USAF/Getty Images; p.23 Bob Gomel/Time & Life Pictures/Getty Image; p.11 Mandel Ngan/AFP/Getty Images; p.16 Murat Taner/Getty Images; p.10 The White House/Getty Images; pp.7 (background), 13 (top), 22 The Granger Collection, NYC/The Granger Collection; pp.9 (background), 15 (top), 25, 31 iStock; pp.10–11 Lexa Hoang (illustrations); pp. backcover & pp.7 (right) LOC, LC-USZ62-48930; p.8 (right) LOC, LC-DIG-ppmsca-23759; p. 8 (left) LOC, LC-USZC4-1495 The Library of Congress; p.19 (bottom) Ben Stansall/AFP/Getty Images/Newscom; p.21 (right) Reuters/Newscom; pp.3, 19 (top) Rorger L. Wollenberg/UPI/Newscom; p.15 (bottom) North Wind Picture Archives; p.13 (both bottom) Michelle Ong; p.17 The U.S. Naitonal Archives; pp.20–21 Wikipedia Commons; all other images from Shutterstock.

Library of Congress Cataloging-in-Publication Data

Rodgers, Kelly.
  Our nation's capital: Washington, DC / Kelly Rodgers.
    pages cm
  Includes index.
  ISBN 978-1-4333-7362-6 (pbk.)
  SBN 978-1-4333-8844-6 (ebook)
1. Washington (D.C.)—Juvenile literature. I. Title.
  F194.3.R65 2014
  975.3—dc23
                                    2014010305

Teacher Created Materials
5301 Oceanus Drive
Huntington Beach, CA 92649-1030
http://www.tcmpub.com
ISBN 978-1-4333-7362-6
© 2015 Teacher Created Materials, Inc.

Table of Contents

The Heart of Our Nation

Many people travel to Washington, DC, each year. They visit the many **monuments**. They go to the various museums (myoo-ZEE-ums). They walk the bustling city streets. Washington, DC, is our nation's **capital**. Many of our country's leaders work there. It is where the president lives. People gather there to honor our country.

The city is full of history. It has hosted powerful **protests** and pleasant parades. New laws are created there, and big decisions are made. People there have argued about how our government should operate. They have guided our country in ways they believe will make life better for everyone.

a celebration at the Capitol building in Washington, DC

There are places in the city to help us learn about our nation's past. We look to the city to remember how our country began. And we look to it to lead us forward. Washington, DC, is located on the East Coast, but it is the heart of our nation.

This is the Jefferson Memorial in Washington, DC. It honors Thomas Jefferson.

We the People

Planning the City

In 1791, the city was named in honor of George Washington. The "DC" stands for **District** of Columbia (kuh-LUHM-bee-uh). The district was named after explorer Christopher Columbus. It is a **federal** district. This means that the leaders of the country work there. It is not part of any state.

President Washington chose Pierre L'Enfant (pe-AIR LAN-fant) to be the **architect** (AHR-ki-tekt). L'Enfant's job was to plan the new city. When he started, Washington, DC, was a large swamp filled with mosquitoes. But L'Enfant wanted the city to be as impressive as the capitals of Europe.

L'Enfant's plans included government buildings. They were to be the largest buildings in America at that time. He wanted people to see the buildings and think of America as a strong country. He set aside an area for the president to live. He planned parks, streets, and public places for people to gather. He wanted the city to be beautiful and easy to use.

George Washington

L'Enfant's plan for the city

Pierre L'Enfant

Government Buildings

Washington, DC, is home to many government buildings. Our leaders meet in them to make big decisions for our country. The White House, the Capitol building, and the Supreme Court are three of these buildings.

This painting from 1807 shows plans for the east side of the White House.

floor plan of the White House

The White House

The White House is where the president lives and works. It is also the people's house. It belongs to all Americans. Each president knows that he or she can only stay at the house for as long as the people allow. When a new president is **elected** (ih-LEK-tid), that person moves into the White House, and the previous president moves out.

In 1791, President Washington chose the site for the White House. It took eight years to build. John Adams was the first president to live there. During the War of 1812, the British set fire to the White House. It took years to rebuild. During the 1900s, many **renovations** (ren-uh-VEY-shuhnz) were made to the house.

Today, the White House is recognized around the world. It is a symbol of freedom, and it is often people's first stop when they tour Washington, DC.

Why That Name?

The White House got its name because so many buildings around it were built from red brick. The bright white color stood out. It helped the president's house get noticed.

The White House has more than 130 rooms! Many of the rooms in the White House are known by their color. The Blue Room, the Green Room, and the Red Room are all famous rooms in the White House. There are bedrooms for the president's family. There is also a large kitchen. The staff can make dinner for over 140 guests! There is a map room and a library. And of course, there are offices for people to work.

Outside, there is a swimming pool and a tennis court to help the president stay fit. There is even a putting green for the president to practice golf! There are also vegetable gardens to help the president eat healthy.

When **foreign** (FAWR-in) leaders travel to America, they are often invited to the White House. Some of them are invited into the Oval Office. This is where the president works. Many big decisions are made in this room.

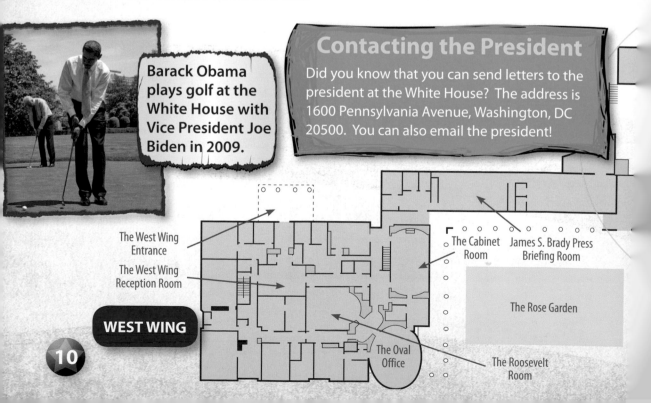

Barack Obama plays golf at the White House with Vice President Joe Biden in 2009.

Contacting the President

Did you know that you can send letters to the president at the White House? The address is 1600 Pennsylvania Avenue, Washington, DC 20500. You can also email the president!

The West Wing Entrance

The West Wing Reception Room

WEST WING

The Cabinet Room

James S. Brady Press Briefing Room

The Rose Garden

The Oval Office

The Roosevelt Room

By the Numbers

The White House is big, but just how big is it? Check out these numbers. There are:

- 412 doors
- 147 windows
- 132 rooms
- 35 bathrooms
- 28 fireplaces
- 8 staircases
- 6 floors
- 1 president

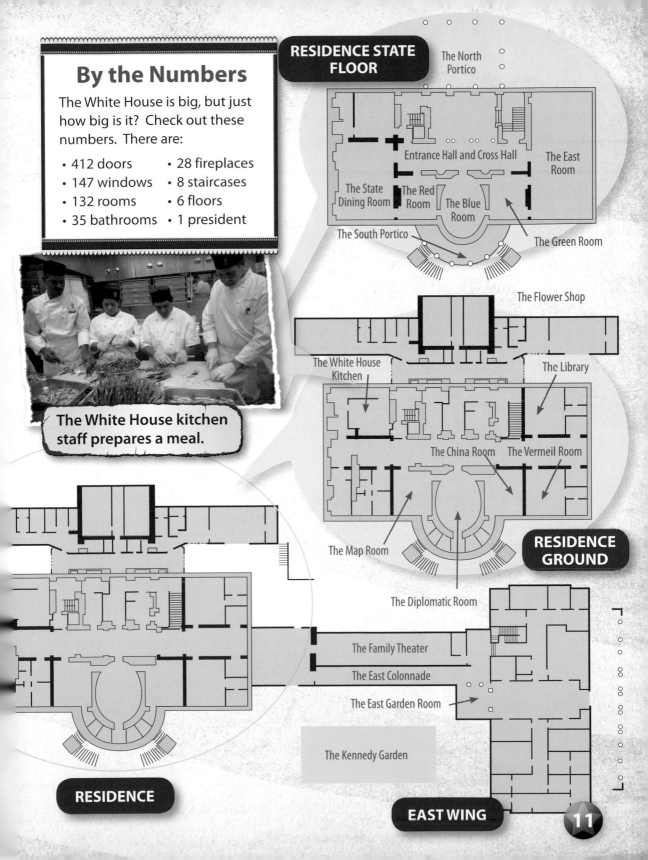

The White House kitchen staff prepares a meal.

RESIDENCE STATE FLOOR

The North Portico

Entrance Hall and Cross Hall

The East Room

The State Dining Room

The Red Room

The Blue Room

The South Portico

The Green Room

The Flower Shop

The White House Kitchen

The Library

The China Room

The Vermeil Room

The Map Room

RESIDENCE GROUND

The Diplomatic Room

The Family Theater

The East Colonnade

The East Garden Room

The Kennedy Garden

RESIDENCE

EAST WING

The Capitol Building

Congress works in the Capitol building. There are hundreds of Congress members. These men and women make sure that the government meets the people's needs. They also write laws. They are chosen by Americans to serve the country.

The Capitol building is in the center of the city. It is a symbol of **democracy** (dih-MOK-ruh-see). This is an American value. It means that everyone should be free to make decisions. A king or queen should not make decisions for us. Everyone should get a say in how the country is run.

Congress in session in 1978

United States Senate

ADMIT

To the Senate Gallery for the One Hundred Twelfth Congress

UNITED STATES
CAPITOL

GALLERY

UNITED STATES

House of Representatives.

ADMIT

To the Visitor's Gallery for the One Hundred Twelfth Congress

UNITED STATES
CAPITOL

HOUSE GALLERY

Seeing It Live

If you plan ahead, you can watch Congress work in the Capitol. Request a free pass to see the government in action.

tickets to watch Congress in session

Building the Capitol was not easy. At times, there was not enough money. Other times, they needed more space. The Capitol building is more than 200 years old. It has survived many changes—even a fire! Today, many people come to admire the statue named *Freedom*. It sits on top of the building.

Statue of Freedom

The Supreme Court

The Supreme Court began in 1790. But it took 145 more years for it to get its own building. Today, it is located near the Capitol building.

The **justices** of the Supreme Court are the highest judges in our country. They have the final word when people do not agree about what a law means. They listen to court cases that are important to the country. Then, they decide which side is right.

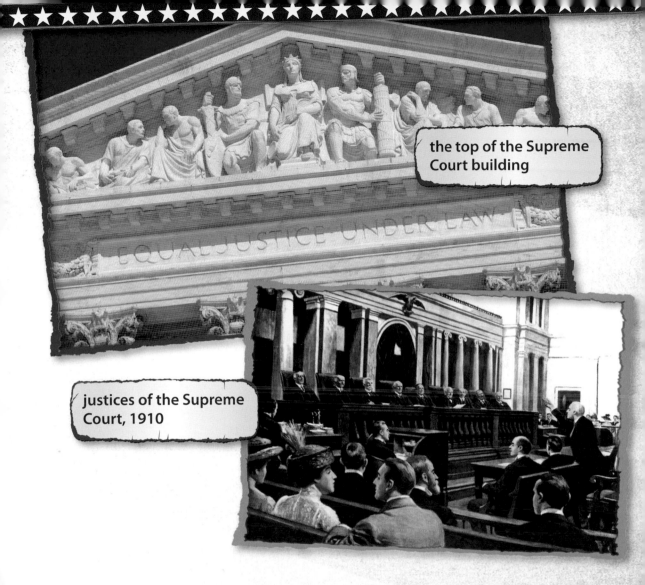

the top of the Supreme Court building

justices of the Supreme Court, 1910

The front of the courthouse has words carved above it. They read "Equal Justice Under Law." This reminds the justices to always be fair. It promises that the Supreme Court is a place where anyone can be heard.

People are welcome to watch court cases. But finding a seat is the hard part! Most of the cases are often very crowded. Some people wait overnight to watch decisions be made.

Places to Learn

There are many places to learn about in Washington, DC. People can find important documents. They can learn about the past. And **scholars** (SKOL-erz) do research to plan for the future.

The Library of Congress

The Library of Congress is the largest library in the world. It has survived fires and wars. Today, the library has 838 miles of shelves! The library collects about two million items per year. It has tons of books and maps. Photos and music are also kept there. It is a place where scholars can learn about any subject.

the Main Reading Room in the Library of Congress

The National Archives

The National **Archives** (AHR-kahyvz) holds our nation's most important records. It has over 10 billion documents! They cover a wide range of topics. They tell when people came to America. They tell who was in the military. They even show when land was bought for America.

You do not have to travel to Washington, DC, to see the library and archives. Just go to their websites. You can study a piece of history from your home!

Buying Alaska

The Library of Congress has an old check written for the purchase of Alaska. It is dated August 1, 1868. The United States paid Russia $7.2 million for the land.

The Smithsonian

Imagine a place where the world's top thinkers could come to trade ideas. What if they could study the latest technology there? Or they might want to see pieces from America's past up close. A museum is a great place to do these things. And the Smithsonian is one of the greatest museums in the world.

Scholars visit the Smithsonian to do research. Some of the nation's best scientists work there. They study everything from the stars in the sky to new animals found in the rain forest.

The Smithsonian is the world's largest museum and research center. It is actually made up of 19 museums! There are several art museums. There is a zoo and a garden. There is a place to learn about the postal system. The collection has over three million items! Protecting these items is important. They help us remember the past and understand the present.

The space shuttle *Discovery* is on display at the Smithsonian.

Shoes and a Hat

The American History Museum at the Smithsonian has a hat worn by President Lincoln. It also has a pair of ruby slippers. Judy Garland wore these famous shoes in the movie *The Wizard of Oz*.

the Smithsonian Natural History Museum

Geology, Gems & Minerals

Ancient Seas Ice Age

Places to Remember

The National Mall is a favorite place to visit in Washington, DC. It is home to special monuments. And it is rich with history. Large groups of people have gathered here to protest unfair laws. Others have come together to support one another.

The White House and the Capitol building are on the Mall. The Mall also includes presidential (prez-i-DEN-shuhl) **memorials**. There are statues honoring those who have fought in wars. There are parks and gardens. The Mall is a symbol of our past. It is a place where Americans come to celebrate the future.

the National Mall

The Washington Monument

The Washington Monument honors America's first president, George Washington. It is a tall, simple statue covered with white marble. It took 36 years to build and was finished in 1884. Around the monument are 50 flags. There is one for each state. The monument can be seen from miles away.

An Obelisk

The Washington Monument is an obelisk (OB-uh-lisk). An obelisk is a tall column. It becomes narrower at the top and ends in a point.

There are 50 flags around the bottom of the monument.

The Lincoln Memorial

You may have seen this memorial before. It is on the back of a penny! The Lincoln Memorial honors President Abraham Lincoln. It was built in 1922. It is larger-than-life, much like our sixteenth president.

Lincoln was president during the Civil War. He wanted to end slavery. He thought slavery was wrong. He was a strong leader, and he helped keep the country together. His work was important to many people. Some started honoring Lincoln with statues and paintings while he was still president!

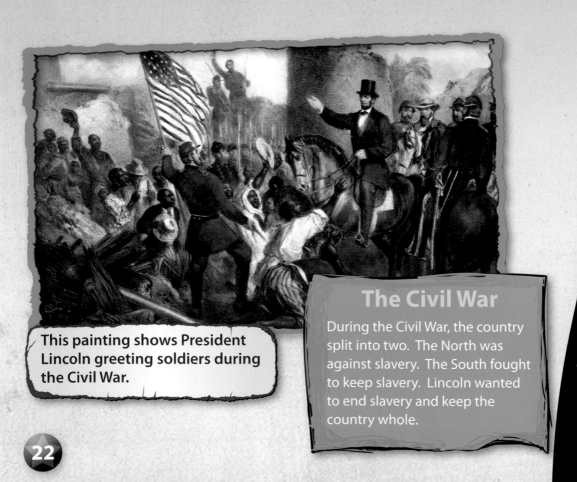

This painting shows President Lincoln greeting soldiers during the Civil War.

The Civil War

During the Civil War, the country split into two. The North was against slavery. The South fought to keep slavery. Lincoln wanted to end slavery and keep the country whole.

People gather in front of the Lincoln Memorial to hear Dr. Martin Luther King Jr.'s speech in 1963.

Many well-known people have spoken at the Lincoln Memorial. Dr. Martin Luther King Jr., gave his famous "I Have a Dream" speech there. He said that all people should be treated the same. It was a powerful place to say these words. He knew that Lincoln had felt the same way nearly 100 years before. Dr. King wanted to link his work with Lincoln's. This made his message even stronger.

The Vietnam War Memorial

From 1954 to 1975, America fought a difficult war. The Vietnam (vee-et-NAHM) War Memorial honors the people who died in this war. It is made of polished stone. The names of the men and women lost in the war are carved into the wall. Visitors often rub the names of those they lost onto paper. In this small way, they can bring part of the memorial home with them.

Name Rubbings

Visitors often find the name of a loved one on the wall. They place a sheet of paper over the name. Then, they take a pencil and rub the paper. The name will then transfer to the sheet of paper.

Vietnam War Memorial

Martin Luther King Jr. Memorial

In 2011, America honored Dr. Martin Luther King Jr. He made America a more equal place. He became a symbol of hope and freedom for many. Today, his memorial helps people remember him. His words are carved into the memorial. They say *Out of the mountain of despair, a stone of hope.* The Martin Luther King Jr. Memorial is the first memorial on the National Mall that does not honor a war, a president, or a white man.

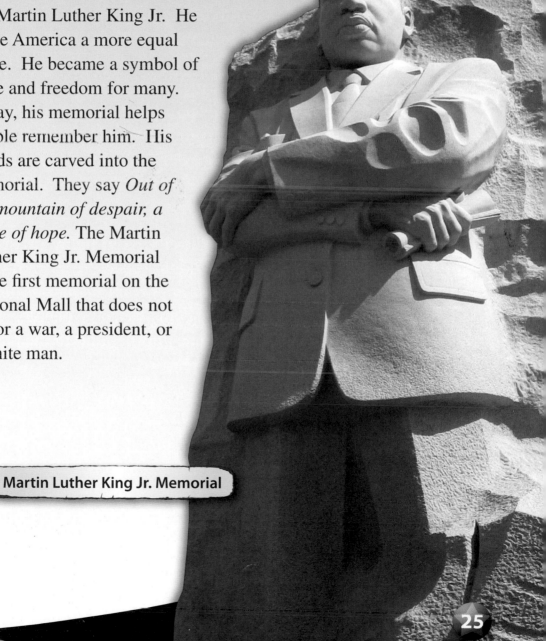

Martin Luther King Jr. Memorial

An American Treasure

Washington, DC, was built to be the home of America's leaders. But it has become so much more. Today, millions of people call Washington, DC, home. People from around the world live there. They bring new ideas and new ways of doing things with them. More than 170 countries have offices there. This is where leaders from other countries work. Students come from all over to attend school there. Many visitors come to Washington, DC, each year. They enjoy the many sights and sounds of the city.

America's past is preserved in the city. And today, artists and historians celebrate it. Lawmakers respect the city. It is home to some of the country's most important memorials and buildings. Its monuments and museums welcome people. They help Americans feel connected to one another and to the past. Washington, DC, is an American treasure.

People gather at the Lincoln Memorial to see the inauguration of Barack Obama.

Plan It!

   A visit to the nation's capital is exciting. Review the places in this book. Make a list of the places you would like to see in Washington, DC. Consider how much time you might want to spend at each site. Make a schedule. Then, add up the times to decide how long your trip should be. Be sure to include time to eat and sleep!

This family examines the U.S. Constitution (kon-sti-TOO-shuhn) at the National Archives.

This family visits the Smithsonian.

Glossary

architect—a person who designs buildings or cities

archives—places where public records or historical documents are stored

capital—a city where the main offices of a government are located

Congress—the group of people who are responsible for making the laws of a country

democracy—a form of government in which people choose leaders by voting

district—an area that has a special purpose

elected—chosen by voting

federal—relating to the central government

foreign—located outside a particular place or country

justices—judges in the Supreme Court

memorials—things that honor a person who has died or serve as a reminder of an event in which many people died

monuments—buildings, statues, or places that honor people or events

protests—events at which people gather together to show strong disapproval about something

renovations—changes and repairs to put something back in good condition

scholars—people who study a subject for a long time and know a lot about it

Index

WITHDRAWN
FROM THE COLLECTION OF
THE BRYANT LIBRARY

Your Turn!

Dear President

Write a letter to the president of the United States. Tell the president why you would like to visit Washington, DC. Ask the president questions you have about what it is like to live there.